The ancient Greeks' world

In ancient times the Greek world stretched further than it does today – there were Greek cities as far apart as Spain and Turkey. Some famous Greek places are marked on this map. See if you can work out which is which. Read the clues and match them up with the pictures, then write the names on the dotted lines.

Athens was an important and powerful city. Its emblem was the owl; this was also the symbol of Athena – the patron goddess of the city.

Mount Olympos is the highest mountain in Greece. The Greeks thought that the gods lived on its peak.

Mycenae was a fortified town on a hill, where the famous king Agamemnon had his palace.

Knossos was the home of the Minotaur, a strange beast with the body of a man and the head of a bull.

Olympia was the home of the first Olympic Games. The ancient Greeks held the games there every 4 years.

At **Delphi** there was a temple to which people came from all over Greece to ask the god Apollo for advice. You can still see the ruins there.

When the Greeks besieged the city of **Troy** the strong walls kept them out for 10 years. At last they managed to capture it when they hid inside a huge wooden horse.

The town of **Sparta** was famous for its soldiers, who were very tough and hardy.

Greek soldiers won a battle against their enemies, the Persians, at a place called **Marathon**.

The Greeks defeated the Persians again in a great sea battle by the island of **Salamis**.

You can find out more about some of these people and events in this book.

Aegaean Sea

1

The Olympian gods

The ancient Greeks had many different gods and goddesses. The twelve most important were thought to live on Mount Olympos. This is the highest mountain in Greece, and its peak is often hidden in the clouds. You can see some of these gods and goddesses on these two pages.

Can you tell which god is which? Each god or goddess had his or her own special symbols. Join up the dots to see them. Then read the descriptions on the next page for the clues and write in the correct name in the box beside each picture.

Athena was a warrior goddess, wearing a helmet and carrying a spear and shield. She was the patron goddess of Athens and her symbol was the owl.

Hermes was the messenger of the gods. He wore a traveller's cloak and hat and winged sandals; he also carried a special kind of stick called a *caduceus*.

Zeus was the father of the gods. He carried a thunderbolt and sceptre and often had an eagle with him.

Hephaistos was the blacksmith god who taught men to use metal. His symbols were the hammer and tongs, but he also carried an axe.

Apollo was the god of light, music and healing, and he often carried a lyre (a musical instrument). He was also an archer and carried a bow and arrows.

Artemis was Apollo's sister. She was also a hunter and carried a quiver of arrows and a bow. She often had wild animals with her.

Aphrodite

The most beautiful of the goddesses was Aphrodite, the goddess of love and of gardens. What do you think she might have looked like? Draw a picture of her in this space.

Greek dress

Greek clothes were very easy to make and to put on. They were usually just made from a single piece of rectangular material, with no special shaping and very little sewing. On this page you can find out how to make clothes like the Greeks wore.

The most common piece of clothing worn by men and women was like a loose-fitting tunic. It had various names, but the most usual are *peplos* and *chiton*. Over this a heavier tunic or a cloak could also be worn; the cloak was called a *himation*.

The *peplos* was long and was worn only by women. To make your own *peplos*:

1. Take a large piece of material (like an old sheet). Its length has to be your height plus at least 18 inches, and when you fold it in half it should reach from elbow to elbow. Fold over the top 18 inches or so.

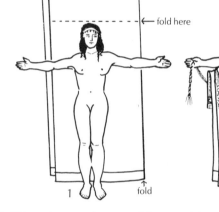

2. Wrap it round you, with one side open. Fasten it at the shoulders with safety-pins or brooches.

3. Tie a belt round your waist. Pull the extra material up so that it hangs over the belt – and so that you don't trip up!

The *chiton* was worn by men and women and could be long or short. To make a *chiton*:

1. For a long *chiton*, the length of the material has to be the same as your height. When you fold it in half it should reach from finger-tip to finger-tip.

2. Sew along the side seam. Join the top edge at intervals with safety-pins or brooches, or by sewing.

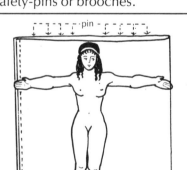

Don't forget to leave holes for your head and arms to go through. Slip it on over your head.

3. Tie a belt round your waist and pull up the extra material so that it hangs over the belt.

A picture to colour. This lady is wearing a *peplos*.

A Greek theatre mask to cut out

Colour this mask and cut it out. Cut round the dotted lines for the eyes and mouth. Pierce the dots at the sides and thread it with elastic so that you can wear it.

This drawing is copied from a bronze sculpture. It shows a tragic mask, but it would not have actually been worn.

A Greek theatre mask to cut out

On the other side of this page is a mask to cut out and wear. You can read more about Greek theatre masks on this page.

The Greeks loved to go to the theatre. Plays were performed during religious festivals and even the poorest people were able to go. Some plays written by Greek dramatists over 2,000 years ago are still sometimes performed today.

In a Greek play there was a chorus and a few actors who would play all the individual parts. The actors always wore masks when they were performing. The masks became more and more exaggerated as time went on — tragic masks got more and more horrific and comic masks more and more ridiculous. The masks would show if the characters were tragic or comic; all actors were men, so if there was a woman in a play a man would take the part wearing the mask of a woman.

There were many different types of mask for showing different kinds of characters — for example, heroes, young women, old women, slaves and so on.

The mask on the other side of this page is for a tragic character. Try to think what a comic mask might look like. Draw it on card and cut it out. Or you could make a mask with the face of a character from your favourite play or television programme.

The Ancient Olympic Games

It was the ancient Greeks who first invented the Olympic Games over 2,500 years ago. They were held at a place called Olympia every 4 years in honour of the god Zeus.

Some of the events would seem quite familiar today – running, discus, javelin, long-jump, boxing. Other events included horse-racing and chariot-racing, as well as wrestling.

One event, like a type of all-in wrestling, was called the *pankration*. The contest went on until one man admitted defeat. In this picture the trainer is about to punish one of the wrestlers for a foul – he is trying to gouge out the eyes of his opponent!

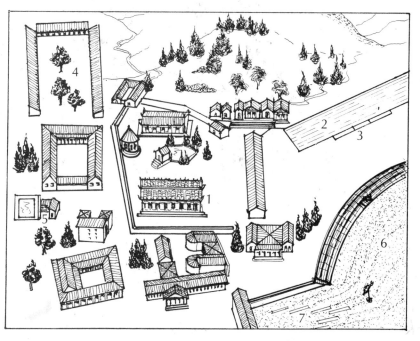

This is a plan of Olympia. Many buildings were added over the years – temples and altars, baths, places where the athletes lived and where they could meet, practise and compete. There was a gymnasium, a hippodrome (for horse-races and chariot-races) and a stadium.

Look on the plan for the numbers and try to find:

1. The temple of Zeus
2. Stadium
3. Judges' stand
4. Gymnasium
5. Baths
6. Hippodrome
7. Starting-gate

Long-jump looked different from the event that we know today. The athlete jumped from a standing position – he was not allowed to take a run up. He held a weight in each hand to help him go further. See how far you could jump like this.

Make a cut-out model of the Olympic Games. First take a large sheet of paper and draw a rectangular track for the stadium and a long thin track for the hippodrome. At each end of the hippodrome there should be a post for the riders and charioteers to turn round. Use matchsticks pushed through the paper for the turning posts.

Colour the figures on the next two pages and cut them out – you can make more by copying them or drawing some of your own. Then arrange them on the sheet to finish your model.

THE PROGRAMME OF EVENTS
included

DAY 1
1. *At the stadium entrance*
trumpeters' competition

2. *In the stadium*
boys' foot-race

3. sacrifice at the altar

DAY 2
In the hippodrome
1. chariot-races
2. horse-races

In the stadium
1. discus
2. javelin
3. long-jump
4. foot-races

DAY 3
In the stadium
foot-races

DAY 4
In the stadium
races in armour

DAY 5
presentation of prizes
feasting and celebration

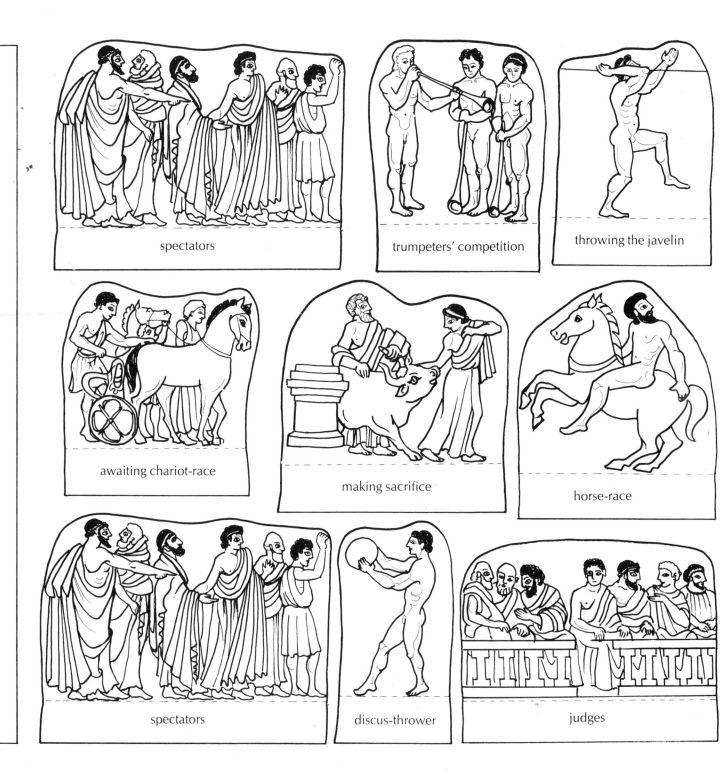

spectators

trumpeters' competition

throwing the javelin

awaiting chariot-race

making sacrifice

horse-race

spectators

discus-thrower

judges

chariot-race

runners

horse-race

javelin-thrower

racing in armour

chariot-race

giving a prize

long-jumper

racing in armour

runners

long-jumper

giving a prize

discus-thrower

The Minotaur's maze

There are many strange creatures in the Greek myths. One of them is the Minotaur, which had the body of a man and the head of a bull. The Minotaur lived in a huge maze at Knossos on the island of Crete. Every year seven youths and seven maidens were sent into the maze by the king of Crete. They either got lost in the maze and starved to death, or were eaten by the Minotaur. No-one had ever escaped. One year the hero Theseus offered to be one of the seven. When he arrived at Knossos the king's daughter Ariadne fell in love with him and decided to help him. She gave him a large ball of string, which he unwound as he went into the maze. Theseus found the Minotaur and killed him with his sword. Then he followed the trail made by the string. Soon he had found his way out of the maze and back to Ariadne, who was waiting for him.

Here is Theseus with the Minotaur in the maze, but where is the string to show him how to get out? See if you can help him to find the way by drawing in the correct path.

The Greek alphabet

capital letter	small letter	letter name	sound
Α	α	alpha	a
Β	β	beta	b
Γ	γ	gamma	g
Δ	δ	delta	d
Ε	ε	epsilon	e
Ζ	ζ	zeta	z
Η	η	eta	e or ay
Θ	θ	theta	th
Ι	ι	iota	i
Κ	κ	kappa	k
Λ	λ	lambda	l
Μ	μ	mu	m
Ν	ν	nu	n
Ξ	ξ	xi	x or ks
Ο	ο	omicron	o
Π	π	pi	p
Ρ	ρ	rho	r
Σ	σ ς	sigma	s
Τ	τ	tau	t
Υ	υ	upsilon	u or oo
Φ	φ	phi	f or ph
Χ	χ	chi	ch
Ψ	ψ	psi	ps
Ω	ω	omega	oh

Answers on page 16

Try writing your name in Greek letters. The table on the left shows you which Greek letter to use for each sound in English. Some English letters are missing. You can see which letters to use instead below:

c use κ j use ι q use κ
v use φ w use ου

To make the sound 'h', use then sign ʿ with the letter. For example ἁ is pronounced 'ha'.

There are two letters for s: use σ at the beginning or in the middle of a word, but ς at the end.

My name is.....................................

ΑΧΙΛΕΥΣ

ΠΕΝΘΕΣΙΛΕΑ

Can you tell which city this coin comes from? The letters at the edge stand for the name of the city, but only part of the word is given. Look at the map on page 1 for another clue.

This coin is from...

You could make coins of your own. Cut out circles of white card. Draw a picture of yourself on one side and write your name round the edge in Greek letters. Choose a special symbol for yourself or the town where you live and draw it on the other side. Write the name of your town round the edge. Then colour it gold or silver.

The picture on the left is a scene from the Trojan War. It was painted on a Greek vase, and it shows the hero Achilles killing the queen of the Amazons. The artist has written their names beside them. Achilles' name is written ΑΧΙΛΕΥΣ. How is the name of the Amazon queen written? Try to write it out in English letters.

....

Greek vase-painting

Most of the jugs, cooking pots and containers used in the Greek household – and even lamps – were made of pottery. The Greeks loved to decorate their pottery with patterns and scenes of people and animals.

The Greeks had special methods for painting pottery called 'black-figure' and 'red-figure' painting. Black-figure vases have their decoration painted on in black and the background is left the colour of the clay – an orangy red. With red-figure vases it is the other way round: the background is painted black and the figures and decoration are left the colour of the clay.

Some vases were even given as prizes in sporting competitions which took place during the Great Panathenaic festival. This was held in Athens every 4 years in honour of the goddess Athena. The vase in the picture on the left was a prize given to a champion boxer at the Panathenaic games. It contained olive oil. On the other side is a picture of Athena and the words: 'I am one of the prizes from Athens'.

On the right is a black-figure vase. To see the effect, colour in the background red. The picture on the vase shows men and boys gathering olives. The men are knocking the olives from the tree by beating the branches with sticks.

The picture on the right is of a red-figure vase. Paint the decoration red and you will be able to see how different red-figure and black-figure painting look. This vase shows a scene at a drinking party. The guests lie back on couches with their drinking-cups, while a woman plays music to them on a pair of pipes.

The pictures on Greek vases were often scenes from daily life and Greek myths. Usually there was a different picture on each side, but sometimes the scene carried on right round the vase. The vase in this picture shows Greeks fighting Amazons. The Amazons were a race of very fierce warlike women. They came to help the Trojans in their war with the Greeks, but their queen Penthesilea was killed by the Greek hero Achilles. You can see a picture of Achilles and Penthesilea on page 11. Try to imagine how this picture might be continued on the other side of the vase.

On the left the vase has been left blank for you to fill in – try finishing the scene of the battle between the Greeks and the Amazons, or make a scene of your own. Colour it in either in red-figure or in black-figure painting. Don't forget to draw in a pattern round the top of the vase – and under the picture, if you like. Here are some of the patterns that you can find on Greek vases to help you:

The Odyssey

The Odyssey is a story that was composed about 2,600 years ago by a man called Homer. It tells of the wanderings of Odysseus, a king of Ithaca who went to fight in the Trojan War. When the war was over, Odysseus set sail for home, but he had many adventures before he returned to Ithaca.

First Odysseus and his men attacked the city of Ismarus, but they were beaten back by the Cicones, who lived there. Then they were blown to the beautiful land of the Lotus-eaters, where the food made all who ate it forget about their homeland.

After this they arrived at the land of the Cyclopes, a race of one-eyed, man-eating giants. The Cyclops Polyphemus trapped them in his cave by placing a huge boulder against the entrance and devoured many of Odysseus' men. But Odysseus gave Polyphemus strong wine to drink and the Cyclops soon fell into a drunken sleep. Then with a sharp stick Odysseus blinded him. The next morning the Cyclops let his sheep out to graze, but he could not find Odysseus and his men. How did they get away?

When the enraged Cyclops realised that Odysseus had escaped, he called on his father, the sea-god Poseidon, to prevent him from reaching home safely.

Later Odysseus and his men rested on the island of Aeolia. To help them on their journey, Aeolus, the king of winds, tied up all the contrary winds in a goatskin. However, Odysseus' foolish crew thought that the goatskin had hidden treasure in it and opened it. The winds rushed out and the ships were blown right back to Aeolia.

At their next stop, Odysseus' men were pursued by giant cannibals. They fled to their ships and rowed with all their might, but the giants hurled great boulders at the ships. What happened then?

Only Odysseus' ship survived. It came to the island of Aeaea, where the sorceress Circe lived. She gave Odysseus' men food, but it had a powerful drug in it which made them forget about their home. Then she waved her magic wand and turned them all into pigs! The god Hermes gave Odysseus a special herb to protect him from Circe's magic and told him how to get the better of her. How did Odysseus make Circe do as he wanted?

Circe released his men. She fell in love with Odysseus, and he stayed with her for a year.

Odysseus' next encounter was with the Sirens — strange creatures that were half woman, half bird. Their beautiful singing lured sailors to their deaths on the rocks. Odysseus' crew stopped their ears, but Odysseus wished to hear their song, so he had himself bound to the mast and listened, while they sailed past in safety.

Next they had to pass through a narrow strait with the Scylla on one side and Charybdis on the other. The Scylla was a fearful monster with 12 feet and 6 ferocious heads, each with 3 rows of sharp teeth. When a ship passed close to her she would snatch 6 of the crew. Charybdis was a terrible whirlpool and any ship sucked into it was lost. Odysseus preferred to steer close to the Scylla's rock and lost 6 of his best men to the monster.

What do you think the Scylla looked like? Draw a picture of her.

Then they came to the island where the cattle of the sun-god grazed. The hungry crew had nothing to eat, so in the end they slaughtered some of the cattle for food. But the sun-god was angry and asked Zeus to punish them. A terrible storm was sent down and their ship was driven right into Charybdis. As it was sucked down Odysseus grabbed an overhanging branch. Later he clung to one of the ship's shattered timbers and floated on the tide.

At last he came to the island of the beautiful goddess Calypso. She fell in love with Odysseus and kept him beside her for 7 years, although he wished to go home. In the end the gods told Calypso that she must let him go. So sadly she helped Odysseus to build a raft and away he sailed. But Poseidon had still not forgotten his anger and whipped up a raging storm to destroy the raft. Luckily a sea-goddess, Ino, took pity on Odysseus and gave him a magic veil. The raft was shattered and Odysseus was forced to swim, but the veil protected him in the mountainous seas, and he reached the shores of Phaeacia.

When they had heard his tale, the Phaeacians agreed to take Odysseus by boat to Ithaca. But although he was home at last Odysseus' troubles were not quite over. For 19 years Odysseus' wife Penelope had waited patiently for his return, but she had many suitors. They wished for her to choose another husband, but she said that first she had to weave a shroud for Odysseus' father Laertes. Every night she unpicked all the work that she had done during the day. At last the suitors became suspicious and Penelope had to finish the work. The time had come for her to make her choice, but she decided that the suitors must enter a contest showing their strength and skill with a bow and arrow. The suitors all failed the contest, but Odysseus succeeded. Afterwards there was a battle at the palace and all the suitors were killed. Finally Penelope recognised her husband and Odysseus reclaimed his palace and his kingdom.

On the back cover of this book there is a game about the adventures of Odysseus.

A picture crossword

Complete the crossword by filling in the names of the pictures in the correct places. You can find all the pictures somewhere in this book.

Answers for page 11
The coin is from Athens. The letters on the edge of the coin actually stand for *Athenaion*, which means 'of the Athenians'.

The Amazon queen's name is Penthesilea. Read more about Achilles and Penthesilea on page 13.

Devised by Jenny Chattington

Drawings by Mary Firman

Many of the drawings are based on objects in the Department of Greek and Roman Antiquities of the British Museum, and the help of Ian Jenkins in producing this book is greatly appreciated.

10th impression 1994

Typeset by Rowland Phototypesetting Limited, Bury St Edmunds, Suffolk and printed in Great Britain by St Edmundsbury Press Limited, Bury St Edmunds, Suffolk.